John Going

The real presence not transubstantiation, no. II

A sermon

John Going

The real presence not transubstantiation, no. II
A sermon

ISBN/EAN: 9783744745109

Printed in Europe, USA, Canada, Australia, Japan

Cover: Foto ©Lupo / pixelio.de

More available books at **www.hansebooks.com**

THE REAL PRESENCE

NOT

TRANSUBSTANTIATION.

No. II.

A SERMON

BY THE

REV. J. GOING, M.A.,

INCUMBENT OF S. PAUL'S, LORRIMORE SQUARE, WALWORTH.

" Let us forbear on both sides needless and unprofitable disputes. Unless
.ou, Lord, hadst said it, 'This is My Body, this is My Blood,' who would have
ieved it? Unless Thou hadst said, O holy Christ, 'Take, eat; drink ye all of this,'
o durst have touched it?"—Dr. SUTTON, *Prebendary of Westminster*, 1605.

LONDON:

G. PEVERALL, PRINTER, WALWORTH ROAD,

1867,

A SERMON, &c.

"And He took bread, and gave thanks, and brake it, and gave unto them,
ng: This is my Body which is given for you; this do in remembrance of
Likewise also the cup after supper, saying: This Cup is the New Testa-
t in my Blood, which is shed for you."—S. Luke xxii. 19, 20.

ʞ my sermon last Sunday evening, I attempted to show
ι that the doctrine of the Real Presence of our Lord's
ʲly and Blood, in the Holy Communion was taught by
 plain words of Holy Scripture, by the earliest Christian
ters after the Apostles, and by the most eminent
·ines of the English Church.

ʲhis evening I shall endeavour to answer the objec-
ıs commonly brought against this doctrine.

Λnd I suppose the chief one of all, though not the most
dly expressed, is, that men cannot realize—and are
cked by—the idea of their own actual contact with God
o hold Christ in our hands, to receive Christ into our
uths—that at a given moment Christ should be not
·ely outside of us but in us; this seems to men fearful
. shocking, and they start back in amazement and
ad at such a statement.

Iy brethren, nearness to God must always be most
'ul to the soul to which it is not most sweet; but why
uld this particular kind of nearness which God vouch-
·s in Holy Communion be at all specially incredible?—
 suffered men to touch His Body when He was here on
th, and to those who loved Him there was nothing

terrible in the contact. The kiss of Judas was, indee
shocking; but the disciple whom Jesus loved leaned
His Breast at Supper, and in after years dwells upon t
fact that "his hands had handled of The Word of Life."*
The penitent harlot pressed His Holy Feet with those li
that had so often been polluted by the kiss of unholy passic
but now that she was penitent, He suffered even *her*
kiss Him,‡ so that the Pharisee marvelled; moreover ᵥ
believe that " the Father is God, the Son is God, and t
Holy Ghost is God"—therefore, when it is said that t
Holy Ghost dwells in the Christian, it is surely God wl
dwells in him—when S. Paul says, " your bodies are t
Temples of the Holy Ghost,"§ he means surely that t
Holy Ghost is in our bodies, and the Holy Ghost is God·
when the Saviour, speaking of the Holy Ghost, says, "I
dwelleth with you and shall be in you,"‖ He means sure
that there is a Real Presence of God the Holy Ghost

---

* 1 S. John i. 1.

† Let it be observed that it was the same Body, the same Real Objecti
Presence of the Saviour that was touched by Judas and by S. John, and wh
the multitude thronged and pressed Him (S. Luke viii., 43-48), many, no dou
were moved by mere curiosity as they rudely pushed and crowded to be ne
Him—they touched the same Body, the same Real Objective Presence, as t
poor sufferer who said within herself, "if I may but touch His garment I sh
be whole." Her Faith and sense of need did not make His Body more Re
or more really present to her than to them, but the virtue that went out
Him to her did not go out of Him to them, though He out of whom the virt
went was as near and as really present to them as to her.

And so the Presence of Christ's Body, His Real Objective Presence in t
Holy Eucharist, does not depend upon the Faith of the receiver, but it do
depend upon that Faith whether virtue shall go out of Him being present,
strengthen and refresh or heal the soul. Still are the words true, "Daught
be of good comfort, thy Faith hath made the whole, go in peace."

His Presence in the Sacrament of the Eucharist is an *Objective* Presenc
that is, it does not depend upon our inward feelings whether He shall prese
or not, just as it was not the Faith of the poor woman that caused B
Presence in the crowd, though that Faith drew upon her the virtue of B
Presence, which came not to others who were as near Him as she was.

‡ S. Luke vii. 38.   § 1 Cor. vi. 19.   ‖ S. John xiv. 17.

the faithful soul. S. Cyril writes " In those who believe
" in Christ, we say boldly, that there is not a mere guiding
" light from the Spirit, but the Spirit Itself dwelleth in us."*
He says, "the Grace through the Spirit is not distinct from
" the Essence of the Spirit,"† so that it may be said that
He dwells substantially in us, using the word in the sense
in which it is used in the Athanasian Creed, when it is
said " that the Holy Ghost is of One Substance with the
Father and the Son."

But not the Holy Ghost only dwells really in us, for the
Presence of Christ is as truly said to abide in the Christian
as it is said to exist in the Holy Eucharist, though no
doubt in a different mode in us and in It. S. Paul says:
" Jesus Christ is in you except ye be reprobates;"‡ he speaks
of "Christ in us the hope of Glory."§ Christ's own promise
was, "Abide in Me, and I [will abide] in you."|| It may be
that His Presence in the Holy Eucharist is not implied in
the words " Wheresoever two or three are gathered together in My Name," (i.e., by My Authority and in Virtue
of My Apostolic Commission¶), "There am I in the midst
of them," (S. Matt. xviii. 20); but His Presence in some
true and real sense with many persons, in many places,
at the same time, is surely implied. And not only is
this said of God the Son and God the Holy Ghost, but
of God the Father also. S. John writes: "Whosoever
shall confess that Jesus is the Son of God, God dwelleth
in him and he in God;" and again, "He that dwelleth in love
dwelleth in God, and God in him;"** nay, all Three Persons
of the Most Holy Trinity are together spoken of as dwell-
ing in the Christian. "If a man love Me he will keep My

---

* S. Cyril in S. John L. V. C. 21, p. 474.
† S. Cyril Dial 7, p. 698.   ‡ 2 Cor. xiii. 5.   § Col. i. 27.
|| S. John xv. 4.   ¶ As we say in *the name* of the Queen.
** 1 S. John iv. 15, 16.

words, and My Father will love him; and We will come ur
him and make Our abode with him."* Speaking of God t
Father, S. Paul says: "In Him we live and move ar
have our being."† We live in God and God in us, n
merely by influence, but by Essence. Most awful, trul
as well as most precious is this our indwelling in God, ar
His indwelling in us, and the doctrine of the Real Presen
in the Holy Eucharist is no more incredible than *this* de
trine is—there is in both cases an equal, though not
similar, contact of the Spiritual and the Material—tl
Heavenly and the Earthly, and in both cases it is equal
incomprehensible.

Now, if we will bear in mind this Essential Indwellii
of the Father, and of Christ, and of the Holy Ghost,
God's faithful people, this consideration will answer or
of the most common and popular objections to the De
trine of the Real Presence, viz., that it is "physically ir
possible" to God, and that it assigns to Christ as mar
Bodies as there are portions of the Consecrated Elemen
on a given day all over the world. A writer says: "
" the doctrine of the Real Presence be true, then in even
" piece of Consecrated Bread, last Sunday, on the Cor
" munion Tables all over the world there were so mar
" Bodies, whole and entire, of the one Man Christ Jesus.'

But why should not this be so, if the Blessed Sacramer
has divine and heavenly properties? God the Holy Gho:
or God the Son indwelling in individual Christians dor
not do so by being partly in one individual, partly i
others, but each faithful Christian has the Holy Gho:
abiding in him, and has Christ abiding in him, yet this dor
not make many Holy Ghosts, or many Christs, becaus

* S. John xiv. 23.   † Acts xvii. 28.
‡ Transubstantiation or Ritualistic teaching, by the Rev. Robert Tapso
Curate in charge of S. Giles, Camberwell, p. 11.

he mode of His Presence is not according to the laws of natural substance. You would not talk of God as though Part of Him existed in America, and Part in Europe, and Part in Australia, so that a person in America had Part of God, a person in Europe another Part of God, a person in Australia another Part of God, but that none of these persons was in contact with God Whole and Entire "about his path and about his bed, and spying out all his ways;"* this would be Pantheism, which makes God everywhere partly, and nowhere perfectly, but you would speak of the Perfect God as Whole and Perfect in every point of infinite space, and yet you would not say that this multiplied God, or made a fresh God in every point of space. When David says, "If I climb up into Heaven, Thou art there; if I go down to Hell, then Thou art there also; if I take the wings of the Morning, and remain in the uttermost parts of the sea, even there also shall Thy Hand lead me, and Thy Right Hand shall hold me,"† he does not mean that he would find Part of God in each of these places and God Whole and Entire in all these places together, nor does he mean to multiply God, by speaking of Him as Whole and Entire in every place; and so when it is said that Christ, Body, Blood, Soul, and Divinity is present in every piece, nay in every particle, of the Blessed Eucharist, it is because He subsists in It in such a divine mode of existence that you no more multiply His Body by multiplying the places of its existence, than you multiply God by believing Him to be present Whole and Perfect in every point of space.

Certainly they who believe in the Real Presence do not believe that they only receive Part of Christ, and *that* in some material sense—when they receive His Body and Blood in Holy Communion, they *do* believe that by a

---

* Ps. cxxxix, 2.　　　† Ibid vv. 7, 8, 9.

wondrous mystery they receive Him, not part of Him, ar
that not Dead but Living; hence they do not think th
by receiving a larger or smaller piece of the Consecrate
Bread or a larger or smaller sip of the Consecrated Wir
they receive more or less of the Body and Blood of Chris
for they know that as our Article says : " they recei
Him only after a Heavenly and Spiritual manner," and n
after the manner of Earthly substances, which admit of tl
notion of *quantity* and may be *more or less;* they belie
that the two Natures of Christ once united can never 1
divided, and that they are not divided in the Bless
Eucharist, but that He is received in It Whole and Entir
both in His Godhead and His Manhood, for to receive Hi
cannot be to receive *Part* of Him. He said : " This is M
Body," not " This is Part of My Body."

As it was on Earth, so now in Heaven, His Presence
Earth was when, and where, and how He willed; ar
now that He is in Heaven, He tells us when, and whe
and how He wills to be present with us, viz., in the Ho
Eucharist; I make no attempt to explain the manner
His Presence, I only resist those who say It is not ther
we do not define, we only assert truth and reality instea
of fiction and shadow, when we speak of a Presence whi
is not the less Real because it is wholly Supernatural ar
Spiritual; and will men dare to call this Presence, whi
is a Divine Presence, a physical impossibility ?

Physical impossibility! What was the whole course
His Ministry on Earth but a proof that physical imposs
bilities were not impossibilities to Him; to feed 4,000 wi
seven loaves, and 5,000 with five loaves, was a physic
impossibility, but not to Him. His Birth was a physic
impossibility, His Fasting forty days and forty nights w
a physical impossibility. His Resurrection from the dea
was a physical impossibility. His Ascension into Heave

was a physical impossibility. God forgive the man that talks of physical impossibility at the Hands of Almighty God.

The writer already referred to boldly declares that the Real Presence of Christ's Spiritual Body in the Holy Eucharist is "a physical impossibility : "* and he says " We " are not bound to believe anything which is opposed to " the evidence of our senses, anything which in itself, in " the nature of *things*," (what things, I ask, material things or spiritual ?) " *is* impossible."†

It would have been but becoming modesty, when contradicting Holy Scripture, and the universal and, as yet, undivided Church, to have said *seems* impossible ; but let me ask who gave Christians of the 19th century this special exemption from all need of believing what seems impossible, when the whole creed of Christians in the 1st century was made up of physical impossibilities ?

It is not a question of possibility, but a question of evidence, and the evidence is triumphant, if only men had faith to receive it. But men call this Transubstantiation,

---

* Rev. R. Tapson as above, ibid.

† S. Chrysostom, Hom. 82, S. Matt.—"Let us in everything believe God, and gainsay Him in nothing, though what is said seems to be contrary to our thoughts and senses, but let His word be of higher authority than both reasoning and sight. These let us do in the Mysteries also, for His Word cannot deceive. Since then the Word said, "This is My Body," let us both be persuaded and believe, and look at it with the eyes of the mind. For Christ hath given us nothing sensible, but, though *in things sensible*, yet all to be perceived by the mind."

Some draw a distinction between what is above reason and what is contrary to reason, and say we are bound to believe many things above reason but nothing contrary to reason.

But little is gained by this distinction, for each person decides for himself that what he himself believes is not contrary to, but only above, reason, and that what he disbelieves is not above, but contrary to, reason.

After all, does not contrary to reason mean contrary to experience, for how can we reason where we have no experience ; but our experience is limited to material things, we have no experience of the powers of spiritual substances.

and plume themselves on not being able to see any difference
between Transubstantiation and the doctrine of the Rea
Presence. As well might a man boast of being blind
Cranmer saw the distinction; Luther and Melancthon saw
the distinction; and on the opposite side the Council of
Trent saw the distinction; the 13th Session of that Council.
Chap. i., is entitled "De Reali Præsentiâ"—"of the Real
Presence." Other subjects are treated of in the intervening
Chapters; and it is not till the fourth, headed "De Transub-
stantiatione"—"of Transubstantiation," that the latter doctrine is considered. Cranmer, no doubt, ended by denying
the doctrine of the Real Presence, as well as the doctrine
of Transubstantiation; but he made a separate recantation
of the one and the other. He says : " This, I confess of myself, that not " long before, I was in that error of the
Real Presence, as " I was many years past in divers other
errors, as of Transubstantiation,"* &c. About ten years
before, in a letter to Cromwell, relating to one of his con-
temporaries, he had said of this person, " that he had ever
" confessed the Very Body and Blood of Christ to be pre-

I suppose it is because we know that we have no such experience that we
accept the doctrine of the Holy Trinity, for in relation to material substance,
trinity and unity in the same substance would be a contradiction, but in the
absence of experience as to Spiritual substance, most of all as to the Self-existent
Substance of the Godhead, we dare not pronounce the doctrine contrary to
reason, and we accept it from Revelation as above reason. But the statements
of Revelation and of the Early Church are far more precise and distinct about
the doctrine of the Real Presence than about the doctrine of the Holy
Trinity, except that the former doctrine implies the latter. Certainly if we
judged by the experience we have of material being, we should pronounce the
doctrine of the Incarnation to be contrary to reason, but as we know not the
powers of the Divine Substance, whereby It might attach to Itself the substance
of Human Flesh, we pronounce that mystery to be not contrary to, but above,
reason. And why can we not do the same in the case of the mystery of the
Holy Eucharist? to reject the doctrine of the Holy Eucharist after having
received the doctrine of the Holy Trinity and the doctrine of the Incarnation,
is to accept the greater mysteries and stop short at the lesser.

* Cranmer's answer to Gardiner, quoted by Goode on the Lord's Supper, p. 46.

" sent in the Sacrament of the Altar, and had only con-
" futed the opinion of the Transubstantiation, and therein
" (he added) I think that he taught but the truth."*

You will have observed that, in the extracts given from
the works of the great English Divines in my last sermon,
the distinction between Transubstantiation and the Real
Presence is clearly marked.

But I may be asked to express in my own words what
the distinction is: and here I would say that the word
Transubstantiation relates only to the outward elements,
and declares that their substance is abolished at the
moment of Consecration; the word Transubstantiation
seems to assert something about the Body and Blood of
Christ, but, in fact, it only denies the existence of the substance of the Bread and Wine. The Real Presence of Christ
is not less real because the substance of the Bread and Wine
remains than it would be if we supposed them to be re-
moved, and the Real Presence may be as firmly believed
on the one supposition as on the other.

If I enter one of the large warehouses of this great City,
and see various kinds of goods stored in casks around me,
and my guide, pointing to them, tells me, "this is flour, and
this is sugar, and this is spice, and this is wine," I only
see the wooden casks, it is true, but yet I do not understand my guide to mean that, in any case the *wood of the
cask* is flour, or sugar, or spice, or wine, still less that what
is there is *only wood*, and nothing beside, least of all, that
when he said "this is flour," he meant there was *no flour
at all in it*, nor do I value the flour the less because I know
the wood is there; and no one would say to me " you do
not understand your guide *literally*, unless you understand
that the wood has been turned into flour, because he said

---

* Jenkyns pref. to Cranmer's Works, i. lxxv.

'this is flour;' and if you once depart from the literal, it would be as natural to believe that the cask is solid wood *through and through*, and has no flour at all in it, as to believe that there was any wood at all, because it was not *all* wood;" yet men have said and do say, if you deny Transubstantiation you must also deny the Real Presence, which is as good as saying, if you deny the wood of the cask to be flour, because he said "this is flour," you must go on to deny there was *any flour at all in it*, because the wood is there. As has well been said, we talk of "stirring the fire, drawing near the fire," when we mean the coals that are on fire—" we drop the mention of the outward " part which contains the fire, and without which the fire " could not be, because it is from the fire contained in " them that we gain warmth. Why then should it be " thought a strange thing that Christians, full of loving " faith, ceased to speak of the outward elements, and only " spoke of That through Which Christ dwelt in them and " they in Christ?"* and this would be especially the case in fervent acts of devotion, when you cannot stop to think about the outward elements, for your whole soul is wrapped up in the thought of the Inward Presence, and you think not and speak not of the bread and wine; hence it is that most of the early Fathers say nothing at all about the bread and wine after the Consecration, as is also the case generally in our own books of devotion; but that is not because the existence of the elements is not believed, but because it is for the time forgotten—the less is swallowed up in the greater. But it would be strange indeed if, when writers speak of nothing but the Inward Thing, we should suppose them to mean nothing but the outward.

And so, the early Christian writers, intent only on the

---

* Pusey's answer to Mr. Goode, Preface p. xx.

Inward Gift, frequently omit any reference to the existence of the outward elements after Consecration, but there is abundant proof that they believed them to remain in their natural substance.

S. Chrysostom, arguing with Heretics, who denied the permanent existence of the Two Natures in Christ, writes : " For as we call the bread, before it is sanctified, bread : " but when Divine Grace has, through the intervention of " the priest, sanctified it, it is set free from the name, " bread, and thought worthy to be called the Lord's " Body, *although the nature of bread remains*, and we pro- " claim not two bodies, but the one Body of the Son ; " so here, too, the. Divine Nature having come to indwell " in the Body, they have together formed one Son, one " Person."*

Theodoret writes (about A.D. 420) : " For neither after " the Consecration do the mystic symbols depart from " their own *nature* : for they remain in their former " *substance* and figure and form, and can be seen and " touched as before ; but in thought they are conceived, " and believed, and adored, as being those Things which " are believed."†

Towards the close of the same century (A.D. 492), S. Gelasius, the Pope of those days, writes : " Certainly the " Sacrament of the Body and Blood of Christ, which we " receive is a Divine Thing, wherefore also we are by the " Same made partakers of the Divine Nature ; and yet *the* " *substance and nature of bread and wine ceaseth not to be*."‡ Who can say how much it might tend to heal the wounds which rend the Body of Christ, His Church, if the Pope of the present day would say the same.

---

* Opp. T. iii. p. 774, ed. Ben.   † Dial. 2 Inconf. p. 125, ed. sch.
‡ De duabus in Christo Naturis, adv. Eutychen et Nestorium, Bibl. Patr. viii. 703.

S. Ephrem, Patriarch of Antioch, A.D. 526 (who wrote against the Nestorians and Eutychians, and died in the year of the fifth General Council), writes: "Thus also the "Body of Christ, which is received by the faithful, *departeth* "*not from the sensible substance*, and remains inseparable "from the invisible Grace."*

Of the same character is the language of Facundus (A.D. 540), in the same Church of which S. Gelasius was a native: "The Sacrament of His Body and Blood, which "is *in* the consecrated Bread and Cup, we call His Body "and Blood, not that the Bread is properly His Body, or "the Cup His Blood, but because they contain *in* them the "mystery of His Body and Blood."†

You will see, therefore, that I do not reject the doctrine of Transubstantiation, because I suppose it to be impossible —for with God all things are possible—but I reject it because the natural sense of words as used in daily life does not show it to be in Holy Scripture, while the same natural sense of words *does* teach the Real Presence, for surely "This is My Body," cannot mean "This is not My Body." And it is not on my own authority that I reject Transubstantiation; I would not dare to do so; I have shown you that I have the authority of the early Christian writers for doing so.

My Brethren, I can say most truly that the word Transubstantiation does not express my belief in the Doctrine of the Real Presence, nor that of any Clergyman of the English Church with whom I am acquainted.

I have read, indeed, that an anonymous writer, calling himself an "English Churchman," has published a book called "Transubstantiation, or, Thoughts on the change

---

* *See* Doctrine of the Real Presence from the Fathers, by E.B. Pusey, D.D., p. 89.

† Pro defens 3; Capp. L. 9; C. 5; Bibl. Patr. x. 79.

consequent on Consecration in the Lord's Supper;" and
the fact that this nameless individual has chosen this title,
has been brought forward as a proof that the whole of
what are now called the High Church party in the Church
of England hold the doctrine of Transubstantiation.   I
have read the book in question, and I think I may say
that the writer above referred to who says "it has just
come into my hands"* had not read it before he used
it as a proof that we all believe in Transubstantiation.
It is a pity that he had not read it, before he quoted it,
or if he had read it he would have found in the first place
the most candid confession from the author that he was
no Theologian—certainly he would have found no evidence
that he was a clergyman, and, what is more important,
he would have found that this person conceived that his
mission was to teach the whole High Church party that
they ought to teach Transubstantiation, which he says they
do not teach, and that it is a great pity they do not teach
it; and this is the witness, and the only witness who is
called to prove that we *do* teach Transubstantiation.†

It is only right however to state that the word Transubstantiation, when first used, had no reference to material
substance, any more than when the Substance of God is
spoken of, and therefore, at least at first, did not carry with
it that gross and carnal meaning which it has acquired in
our ears in modern times; for the word substance, as employed by the schoolmen in their distinction of *substance* and
accidents, applied exclusively to what was immaterial, or, as
we should say, *unsubstantial;* all that we understand by the
term *substance*, as applied to material things, viz., density,
weight, color, form, taste, quantity, *i.e.*, the capacity of

* Rev. R. Tapson (as above), p. 10.
† See Appendix A, on the Rev. R. Tapson's Misquotations.

being more or less—they understood by the term accident and *excluded all these from their idea of substance.** †

I cannot myself conceive the substance of material things as distinguished from their accidents to be anything but a fanciful and unreal notion, having no existence at all; but certainly it is not a gross or carnal notion.

This so-called substance it is, however, which was said to be changed into the substance of the Body and Blood of Christ, the accidents, or what we should call the substance, remaining unchanged. This was the original meaning of the word Transubstantiation, and in this sense ‥ believe many of the greatest divines of the Roman Church still use it.‡ Would to God that they all did !

---

* See Wilberforce on the Incarnation, note to chapter x.

† Consubstantiation was a term of ridicule applied by Roman Controversialist to the followers of Luther as expressing their belief, but the Lutherans always protested against the term as not expressing their belief, and justly, for Consubstantiation does not mean the co-existence of *diverse* substances, else you could not say that the three Persons of the Blessed Trinity are Consubstantial with each other, as the Church has always taught.

Diverse substances could only be Consubstantiated by *confusion* of substance whereby two diverse substances become one common substance ; but this was not what the Lutherans taught. They did not teach that the substance of bread was *blended* with the Body of Christ.

I suppose no one would say that because our Lord was both God and Man the Godhead and the Manhood co-existing in One Person, therefore His Godhead and His Manhood were *Consubstantiated.* To say this would be the heresy of the Eutychians, which is condemned in the Athanasian Creed ; when speaking of our Saviour it says that His Godhead and His Manhood are "One " altogether, *not by Confusion of Substance* but by *unity of Person.*"

" To say that our Lord's Body was 'Consubstantiated' with the bread, would " be the blasphemy of saying that It was united with the bread into one " Common Substance."† Whatever other errors the Lutherans may have taught (see note, p. 38) they never taught *this,* and certainly the English Church has never taught it.

† E. B. Pusey, D.D., Presence of Christ in the Holy Eucharist, p. 15.

‡ I may add that no doubt it is for this reason that the greatest living divine of the English Church has expressed the belief that with mutual explanations between the two Churches as to *our* belief in the real Presence, and *their* interpretation of the word Transubstantiation, this doctrine need not prevent the intercommunion of the two Churches.

From this it will be seen that the difference between
Transubstantiation and the Real Presence is simply this,
that the former term denies the existence of the substance
of bread and wine as distinguished from its accidents (whatever that may mean), but the word Transubstantiation adds
nothing to the Presence of Christ, which may be equally
Real, whatever be our notion about the substance of the
bread and wine.

It is because Transubstantiation denies the substance of
the Bread and Wine to exist after Consecration, that the
XXVIIIth Article says it " overthroweth the nature of a
Sacrament," for the Church had already defined a Sacrament to be "an outward and visible sign of an inward and
spiritual Grace,"* and it followed that if the bread and wine
ceased to exist in their natural substances, even though they
seemed to be there, the outward and visible sign was gone,
and the nature of a Sacrament was overthrown. Moreover,
such a doctrine is said to be repugnant to the plain words
of Scripture, because our Lord called the Wine which He
had just consecrated the "fruit of the vine,"† and three
times in one Chapter S. Paul calls the Bread which had
been consecrated, and which some ate unworthily, by the
name of " Bread." ‡

Transubstantiation is defined by our Church to be " *the
change of the substance of the bread and wine*," § not the belief
of the Real Presence of Christ in them.

He who allows the Presence of bread and wine in their
natural substances, does not teach Transubstantiation, however strongly he may teach the doctrine of the Real
Presence, nor does our difference with the Church of Rome

---

* Catechism.
† S. Matt. xxvi. 29.   S. Mark xiv. 25.   ‡ 1 Cor. xi. 26, 27, 28.
§ xxviiith Article.

as to the Holy Communion relate at all to the doctrine
the Real Presence but to Transubstantiation, and the wit
holding the Cup from the laity, which I have shown in r
first sermon (pp. 16-17) to be as contrary to the practice
the primitive Church as to the plain teaching of Holy Scr
ture.

I accept with all my heart the Article of the Engli
Church on this subject, and will here give an extract fro
the Catechism of Holy Communion published by a cor
mittee of clergy who may be truly said to represent t
belief of those members of the English Church who a
so loudly accused of holding Transubstantiation.

It puts the question,—" Do the bread and wine cease
" exist after consecration ? "

Answer. " No. The elements continue bread and wi
" as they were before, but they have become what th
" were not before, the Body and Blood of Christ."*

This is the doctrine of the Real Presence as distinguish
from the doctrine of Transubstantiation.†

---

* p. 13.

† The 31st Article is sometimes quoted, as though it implied a disbelief
the doctrine of the Real Presence, whereas what that article denounces is t
shocking belief which was prevalent among the people at the time the Arti
was written, and which was no doubt widely encouraged by many of the prie
for their private gain, viz., that remission of pain and guilt could be obtained
even the most wicked persons, if only a sufficient number of masses were s
for the repose of their souls. History leaves no doubt that this was the popu
belief of that time; this is what " was commonly said," as the Article hath
and enormous sums of money were paid for such superstitious masses. Su
doctrines and practices are rightly called " blasphemous fables and dangerc
" deceits."

But the language of the Council of Trent (Session xxii.) against these sa
practices is scarcely less strong than that of our own Church ; it is
follows : " The Holy Council decrees that the bishops, ordinaries of each pla
" diligently take care and be bound to forbid and put an end to all those thin
" which either *avarice*, which is idolatry, or *irreverence*, which is scarce
" separable from impiety, or *superstition* the pretence of true piety, h

But it is said there is no Real Presence because we ·ead the figurative expressions, " Judah is a lion's whelp ; ' Issachar is a strong ass ; the seven kine are seven years ; ' the field is the world ; the good seed are the children of ' the kingdom; the tares are the children of the wicked one; ' the reapers are the angels. I am the Door ; I am the Vine," .nd so on—and the writer of the above adds, " I go into a ' room of statuary, and, pointing to a bust of Homer or ' Cicero or Napoleon or Nelson, I say, there is Homer, there · is Cicero, there is Napoleon, there is Nelson ; now I run no risk of deceiving or misleading any one by such a form of peech."*   None, certainly !   But can any one say that our

---

introduced, and to say much in a few words, first of all as to *avarice*—let them altogether forbid agreements and bargains of *payment* of whatever kind, and *whatever is given for celebrating new masses*, moreover importunate and mean extortion, rather than petition of alms, and such like practices, which border on Simoniacal sin, certainly on filthy lucre, and let them altogether remove from the Church *a set number of certain masses and candles, which has proceeded rather from superstitious observance than from true religion*, and teach the people in what consists and from whom above all proceeds the so precious and heavenly fruit of this most holy Sacrifice." So many masses, and so any candles to release a soul from Purgatory !

Now it would be as reasonable to infer that because these superstitious masses e denounced by the Council of Trent, therefore that Council denied the Real .esence ; as it would be to make the same inference as regards the English ιurch.

I may add that Alvarus Pelagius, a Roman Bishop in the 14th century, ·ites as follows :—

"Our Church is full and over-full of altars, masses, and sacrifices, and therewith is, in the sacrifices, full of homicides, sacrileges, uncleannesses, and simonies and other wickednesses, excommunications and irregularities to the very ιtmost. For at this day so many masses are said for gain, or custom, or :omplaisance, or to cover wickednesses, or for their own justification, that)oth among priests and people the Holy Body of the Lord is now held cheap. ·And now through custom or rather corruption it has indurated, that a mass ·riced at three or four denars, or one shilling, is bought and sold by a blind -eople and by wicked simoniacal priests." These are the masses denounced the article. Alvarus Pelagius de Planctu Eccl. ii. 5, quoted by Dr. sey in the Eirenicon, p. 29-30.

* Rev. R. Tapson (as above), pp. 13, 14.

Lord ran no risk of teaching the Real Presence when He sa
" This is My Body, This is My Blood," and caused three
His Disciples who followed Him on earth to record His exa
words, and even gave the same words in Heaven, or fro
Heaven, to a fourth Disciple who had not been His Discip
while He was here on earth—I mean S. Paul. People real
speak as if Our Lord *incautiously* used words most likel
to mislead, *and did not perceive that they would mislead.* D
He not *foreknow* that the whole of Christendom, until 3(
years ago, would learn " this soul-destroying heresy" (;
some have called it) *from His words*—what millions
souls misled for 1,500 years, what millions still misled
Could not He, who foresaw all things from the beginnin
have chosen less perilous terms where the risk was so tr
mendous ? If it were a deception to believe in the Re
Presence, I think I have proved to you in my former se
mon that the whole Church of God was actually deceive
from the very time of the Apostles until a few centuri
back ; and be it remembered, that the writers I quote
testify not to the date only at which they wrote, b
declare that they had been *taught* what *they* taught
others. Certainly there would be no risk of deceivii
any one by such expressions as " this is Napoleon," " I a
the Door," for in the one case there is the *material li*
ness, for the bust is, in substantial form or configuratic
like Napoleon ; in the other, there is the *moral likeness,* f
Our Lord is the Door or opening (thura)* whereby we ent
the Heavenly Kingdom ; and the material likeness in t
one case, and the moral likeness in the other, could not f
to guide the hearer to Our Lord's meaning; but when He sa
of the bread " This is My Body," there was neither t

---

* θύρα.

material nor the moral likeness to guide the hearer, for of course the bread was not like our Lord's Body materially, and if He had meant a moral likeness He must have reversed the order of His words, omitting the word "this," and said, "My Body is bread for the soul," not "*this* bread is My Body which is given for you." My brethren, what I said before I now repeat, there is no theory to which Our Lord's words may be made to fit, according to any natural use of language, but the theory of the ancient undivided Church—the doctrine of the Real Presence as distinguished from Transubstantiation.

Then again Holy Communion is said to be a Memorial, and it is alleged that the memorial of a thing cannot be the thing itself; but a memorial may be a memorial in the way of *identity*, as well as in the way of *likeness*. Was not the manna, which was laid up for a memorial* in the Tabernacle of the Lord, *the thing itself of which it was to be the memorial for all generations,* and is it not the very type of our Lord's Body, as referred to by Him in the VIth Chapter of S. John. The memorial of an offering is a very frequent expression in the Books of Moses: "He that hath sinned shall bring for his offering the tenth part of an ephah of fine flour for a sin offering, he shall put no oil upon it, neither shall he put any frankincense thereon, for it is a sin offering; then shall he bring it to the priest, and the priest shall take *his handful of it, even a memorial thereof,* and burn it on the altar, according to the offerings made by fire unto the Lord, it is a sin offering."† Of the Meat Offering it is said "He shall bring it to Aaron's sons, the Priests, and he shall take thereout his handful of the flour thereof, and of the oil thereof, with all the frankincense thereof, and the Priest shall burn the

---

* Exodus xvi. 33, 34.   † Lev. v. 11.

memorial of it upon the altar, to be an offering made by fi
of a sweet savour unto the Lord, and the *remnant* of tl
meat offering shall be Aaron's and his sons, it is a thir
most holy of the offerings of the Lord made by fire."*

These words, with scarcely an alteration, occur thr
times in that one chapter, (and many times elsewher
and always with the same meaning, the word *memorial* n
meaning a thing to keep in remembrance a past ever
but that small part or "handful" of the offering th
was actually presented to God, and it was termed *mem*
rial because its object was that God in His mercy mig
remember the offerer for good.

" The word *mneemosunon*,† is a sacrificial word, as may`
" seen in Leviticus and elsewhere, as well as the kindr(
" word *anamneesis*,‡ and when so applied means alwa;
" 'something offered to Almighty God to remind Hir
" of the worshipper himself, or of some other person
" object in whom the worshipper takes an interest, or
" His own loving kindness shewn by mercies past
" gracious promises for the future."—*Keble's Euchari*s
Adoration, page 68.

The word *memorial* is used in the same way by t
Angel who spoke to Cornelius and said : " Thy praye
and thine alms are come up for a *memorial* (mneemosuno
before God."§ What more accurate description of the He
Eucharist (if we believe the Real Presence) than "Do tl
(eis teen emeen anamneesin) for *my memorial?*" general
the kindred word *mneemosunon* is employed in the Septu
gint to express *memorial* in this sacrificial sense, but twi(
at least, the word *anamneesis* is employed, which is th
used by our Lord, when he said: "Do this in remembran
of Me."‖ Moses, speaking of the shew-bread (Lev. xxiv. 7

---

* Lev. ii. 2, 9, 16. † μνημόσυνον. ‡ ἀνάμνησις.
§ Acts x. 4. ‖ S. Luke xxii. 19.

writes, " Thou shalt set them (the cakes) in two rows, six on a row, upon the pure table before the Lord, and thou shalt put pure frankincense upon each row, that it may be on the bread for a memorial *(eis anamneesin.)* Even an offering made by fire unto the Lord "—and Numbers x. 10: " Ye shall blow with the trumpet over your burnt offerings, and over the Sacrifices of your peace offerings, that they may be to you for a memorial *(anamneesis)* before your God." The blowing of the trumpet was symbolical of the idea that God's attention was to be called to His people; nay, the very word " do " "this do," is a sacrificial word: Lev. ix. 7. Moses said unto Aaron, " Go unto the altar and *offer* thy sin offering," &c. The word is *(poieeson)* do.* When the Blessed Virgin took her Holy Son to the Temple to " *do* for Him after the custom of the Law,"† the word *poieesai, to do,* means to *offer Sacrifice.*

In the ears of those who heard the words, and were used to the Jews sacrificial language, I doubt not that when the Saviour said : " *touto poieite eis teen Emeen Anamneesin*" " Offer this as My Memorial," He seemed to them to mean, " I am the Sacrifice for the world's sin, and This will be for " ever the *Memorial* of that Sacrifice—the little " handful " " which you can offer to God in the Holy Eucharist—and " thereby you shall offer Me before My Father that you " may be remembered by Him for good."

But even though our Lord may not have used *anamneesis* or *memorial* in the strict sacrificial sense as explained in the law of Moses, it is still true that, even as a remembrance, a memorial may be a memorial in the way of identity, as well as in the way of similitude or likeness, for as I have said above, the manna was the same thing of which it was the memorial—men preserve pieces of the wood of the

---

* πόιησον.   † S. Luke ii. 27.

Royal George as memorials of that ill-fated vessel, and
they are so because they are its *very substance*, and the
Memorial of the Sacrifice of Christ, *even as a Remembrance*,
may still be His Real Body and Blood, supernaturally
present in the Holy Eucharist.

Another objection, though often refuted, has appeared in
the papers in the last few days, viz., that they who believe
in the Real Presence crucify the Redeemer anew at each
repetition of the Sacrament. The author of this state·
ment has since explained himself by saying, that " It is
vain to attempt to retain the reality of Sacrifice and at the
same time to deny the reality of death."*

Certainly it would be a vain attempt, but the death may
take place at one time, and the offering and eating of the
sacrifice at another; what has been said in my last sermon
about the laws of Sacrifice will supply a full answer to this
objection. " They that eat of the sacrifice are partakers of
the altar"—it was the imperfection of the animal sacrifices
of the Mosaic Law that fresh victims needed continually to
be slain to provide afresh, from year to year, means whereby
men could eat of the sacrifice and be partakers of the altar:
it was the perfection of the One Great Sacrifice for sins for
ever, that the Flesh of the Victim once slain abides for
ever that men may eat thereof and not die; like the loaves,
in the miracle of our Lord, that did not grow less as men
ate of them. At last a Victim was found whose Flesh might
be always eaten, and yet never be exhausted; with such a
Victim, what need to talk of a fresh slaying of the
Victim every time His Sacred Flesh is presented to God,
and pleaded before Him for the remission of our sins, and
then fed upon by the faithful soul as really as the Paschal
Lamb was fed upon by the Jew, although after a heavenly
and spiritual manner.

* Hugh McNeile, D.D., letter to the *Times* newspaper, Feb. 21, 1867.

Nor does this hinder the work of Christ from being "*a finished work*," unless by that word we mean that His office as our High Priest came to an end at the moment of His death—nay, rather it was then that He entered on His office in its highest meaning. We must not narrow down to the limits of our Saviour's life on earth the Sacrifice that like a rainbow of mercy spans all time, nor must we deny that it is "a finished work" because it is a *lasting* work, and did not vanish away as soon as it arose; we must not think that He returned to heaven because there was no more left for Him to do for men, but with as definite a purpose as that for which He originally left His Father's throne, viz., to be our High Priest "for ever,"* and with "somewhat also to offer"† on our behalf, viz., Himself. In this sense His work will never be "finished" as long as there are sinners to save and sins to pardon; and the Holy Eucharist on earth is a Sacrifice identical with the perpetual Burnt-offering of Heaven, and not a repetition of the Slaying of the Victim on Calvary.

We do not teach that the priest at the Altar repeats what our Lord did on Mount Calvary upon the Cross, but that what our Lord is now doing in Heaven for men He commands men to do in His Name on earth, and the efficacy of their offering on Earth is derived from the efficacy of His offering in Heaven. It is the same offering.‡ For it is not a dead but a living Christ that we offer, and on whom our souls feed in Holy Communion. Even Luther and Melancthon said this. The Roman Writers had charged the Lutherans with believing in "a dead Christ contrary to the saying of Paul—" 'Death hath no more dominion over

---

* Heb. vii. 21.   † Heb. viii. 3.

‡ *See* Catechism of Holy Communion, p. 12.   Q.—"Is this a fresh offering of Him?" A.—"No, it is the continual presentation of His one Oblation of Himself once offered, and is part of that same offering."

Him,' "* and Melancthon replied, that " In the Supper of
" the Lord, we speak of the Presence of the living Christ,
" for we know that death hath no more dominion over
" Him,"† and in the first imperfect sketch of their Apology
the Lutheran Divines wrote, " We do not feign that the
" dead Body of Christ is received in the Sacrament, or that
" a Bloodless Body or Blood without a Body is received;
" but we hold that Christ Whole and Living is present in
" each Part of the Sacrament."‡ Yet, because they would
not accept Transubstantiation, their explanations were
rejected by the Roman Church.

Yes, my brethren, we do not believe in a dead but a living
Christ in the Holy Eucharist—" we are saved by His life."§
He is made our High Priest " not after the law of a carnal
commandment, but after the power of an endless life." ‖
And this is the answer to another popular objection, that
if the doctrine of the Christian Sacrifice were true *Hiereus*,
ἱἐρευς and not *Presbyter*, πρεσβύτερος would have been
the word to describe the office of the Christian Priest-
hood—if indeed the office of the Christian Presbyter
were to *kill* Christ (God forgive the word, which is not
mine,) then indeed he would have been called Hiereus,
and would share day by day, and week by week, the sin
of the Jews and of Pontius Pilate and of Judas, but as
his office is to offer before the Father Him " who liveth
and was dead, and behold He is alive for evermore,"¶ it
would have been wrong to call him Hiereus, who slays,
it is enough to call him presbyter, of which our word
priest is but an abbreviation, for it is not his name, but His

---

* Can Dr. McNeile have forgotten this fact, when he charges the Roman
Church with professing to kill Christ in the Eucharistic Sacrifice.

† Doctrine of the Real Presence, p. 34.

‡ Apol. Conf. Aug. in Chytr. Hist. Aug. Conf. p. 344, Ed. Lat.

§ Rom. v. 10.   ‖ Heb. vii. 16.   ¶ Rev. i. 18.

Lord's Commission ("This is My Body, do this in remembrance of Me") that invests the presbyter or priest with his office.

Had the Christian Presbyter been called Hiereus, it would have kept up the Jewish notion of animal sacrifice, which the apostles were so anxious to show had come to an end with the death of Christ our Lord.—It would have confused the Christian with the Jewish sacrifice, and destroyed the idea of "one Sacrifice for sins for ever," in which the Hiereus and the Victim were one and the same. The Gentiles, accustomed to the word in their own bloody sacrifices, in which not only animals but sometimes men were slain, would have been utterly confounded, when the Unbloody Sacrifice of the Christian Altar was said to be offered by a man bearing the same name as the offerer of their own bloody, nay, it may be, human sacrifices. In after years, however, when Christianity had triumphed throughout the civilized world, and the danger of confusion with the ideas of heathen or Jewish Sacrifices had passed away, the Greek term Hiereus, and the Latin, Sacerdos, came to be used indifferently with Presbyter or Priest.

Another objection is, that our Lord could not really have imparted His Body and Blood to His disciples in the Holy Eucharist, *because He had not yet died ;* but of course it is obvious that this objection would only apply if we taught a *natural* or *material* Presence—for surely Almighty Power could have as easily imparted the supernatural Presence of His Body and Blood before His death as after it.

And when ignorant people call us *cannibals and idolaters,* the answer is the same. It is only by teaching the natural Presence of Christ's Body and Blood that we could be called cannibals ; but what we teach is a Presence altogether supernatural and Heavenly, but yet real ; and every argument, which proves the Presence to be real, is an answer to the charge of idolatry, for no reverence to Our Saviour really Present could be idolatry, because it is not to the natural substance of the Elements we pay reverence, but to the Supernatural Presence of Our Blessed Saviour's Body and Blood. "No man hath seen God at any time,"* and when Moses bowed down and fell on his face before the Lord, in the cloud,† he did not see God, but yet he paid not his reverence to the cloud, but to Him Whom the cloud hid from his sight but Whom he knew to be there, and we no more worship the Elements than he worshipped the cloud, though we adore Christ Present we know not how.

Idolatry is a sin of intention as much as conspiracy or fraud, or murder is, and as impossible to be committed without intending it as those crimes are; idolatry can only be committed by him who intends to worship as God some creature of God.

But in the case supposed it was never intended to worship the creature, either by those who hold Transubstantiation or by those who hold the Real Presence without Transubstantiation; the one side holds that the creature is abolished, so that there is no creature to worship, but God only; the other holds that the creature remains, i.e., the bread and wine, but worships not them, but that dear Lord who is really Present, though hidden from our eyes by those earthly veils.‡

---

* S. John i. 18. † Exodus xxxiv. 5, 8.

‡ Men say, indeed, that the golden calf which the Jews worshipped in the days of Moses, and the calves which Jeroboam set up at Dan and Bethel, were meant to be images to represent Jehovah, and yet it was sin to worship them as Him; and therefore they argue it is sin to worship Christ really Present in the Blessed Eucharist, even granting His Presence. But first of all, the Jews were strictly forbidden to make any image of God or any supposed likeness for the purpose of worship; now let us for a moment suppose that God had not forbidden this but had really informed them that the image was His Body, He being Present in it in some supernatural way, would it *then* have been a sin for them to worship

An objection is raised against taking our Lord's words in the VIth of S. John in their plain literal meaning, because after His discourse with the Jews, about eating His Flesh and drinking His Blood, He said to His disciples " What and if ye shall see the Son of Man ascend up where He was before, it is the Spirit that quickeneth, the flesh profiteth nothing, the words that I speak unto you they are spirit and they are life."* And is it then seriously pretended that His words are *not* spirit and life to any one who believes in the Real Presence of His Spiritual Body in the Blessed Sacrament—must we disbelieve His words to make them spirit and life to us? were they not spirit and life to the old

---

Jehovah after He had told them that He was in a supernatural way *there*—would it not have been a duty, or rather a religious instinct to do so?

Now no one can contend that the Bread and Wine is a "graven image" of Christ our Lord, or "any likeness" of Him, and He certainly has not forbidden us to worship Him as Present in those elements which He called His Body and Blood, and therefore we may yield to our religious instincts, and worship Him Present in the Blessed Eucharist; it is not commanded "by Christ's ordinance," truly, but there was no need to command what natural piety would prompt, if men only once believed that He was there. May we not be sure that if it had been wrong to worship we should have been mercifully warned from so natural an error.

Great stress is sometimes laid upon the words of the 28th Article, which says, "The Sacrament of the Lord's Supper was not *by Christ's ordinance* "reserved, carried about, lifted up, or worshipped," but because these practices formed no part of Christ's ordinance, it does not follow that they are therefore wrong. Confirmation was not, so far as we know, a thing "ordained by Christ Himself," but it would be a strange inference to argue that Confirmation was wrong because it was not ordained by Christ Himself, or that it is not a grievous loss to the soul and disobedience to God to neglect this holy rite, for, although not ordained by Christ Himself, it was practised by the apostles and their immediate successors.

We have the express testimony of S. Justin Martyr in the second century that one of the duties of a deacon was to carry the Holy Eucharist "to those not present," that is, to the sick or to those in prison for the faith, &c. It must, therefore, have been reserved for that purpose, but this was no part of Christ's ordinance like giving the cup to all—"drink ye *all*" of it—and the plain meaning of the article is that this is not essential. Christ's ordinance was not broken if it were omitted, as in withholding the cup from the laity.

* S. John vi. 62, 63.

saiuts, who lived upon the thought of His Divine Presence in the "life-giving Eucharist," as they called it? this is to make Him contradict His own words which He had just spoken, when in fact He does but confirm them; for He does not say that *His* flesh profiteth nothing, but *the* flesh, which is a term of most frequent use and definite meaning in the New Testament, and always means the Old Adam within us as distinguished from the New—thus it is written " the law was weak through the flesh,"* because the children of the Old Adam could do nothing without the grace of the New Adam. " The flesh lusteth against the spirit so that ye cannot do the things that ye would,"† *i.e.*, the nature

During the reign of King Edward the VIth, the reservation of the Blessed Sacrament was ordered to be discontinued, probably, as some have thought, for fear of the profanities to which It might be exposed at the hands of unbelieving priests, of whom there were many at that unsettled time, and the object of the 28th Article seems to be to deny that this discontinuance of the ancient custom of reserving the Sacrament in any way infringed on Christ's ordinance. In restoring the cup to the laity our Church relied upon Christ's ordinance, and it was necessary to show that, in removing other things, she was not opposing Christ's ordinance, and what has been said about this practice applies to the others mentioned in the Article, viz.—that It was not by Christ's ordinance "carried about, lifted up, or worshipped." These were no part of Christ's ordinance, but it does not therefore follow that they are forbidden.

The lifting up of the Sacrament before the people is a very ancient practice, and is found in nearly all the primitive liturgies; the other practices referred to, the procession and exposition of the Host for worship, are of later date.

From the day of Pentecost Christians have adored not the Sacrament, but our Lord in the Sacrament, but the Church has, at different times, used different ways of expressing her feelings of love and worship. One way was used at one time and one at another, and so our Church was quite justified, on account of the prevalence of superstition and unbelief, in omitting, as of obligation, those very rites whose introduction, in another age, was most pious and commendable.

One proof that the article did not mean to condemn those practices of which it says they were not done " by Christ's ordinance," is to be found in the fact that the Episcopal Church of Scotland, which is, and always has been, in full communion with the Church of England, and which equally accepts the 39 Articles, nevertheless permits the reservation of the Blessed Sacrament.

* Rom. viii. 3.   † Gal. v. 17.

of the Old Adam struggles against the grace of the New.
The expression is so explained in the IXth Article of Religion. Works of depravity are called the "works of the
flesh;"* sinful lusts are termed "the lusts of the flesh,"†
for the flesh of the first Adam was the fountain of sin and
death, the Flesh of the Second Adam, of purity and life,
because "the first man Adam was" only "made a living
soul," possessed of mere natural life; "the last Adam was
made a Quickening or Life-giving Spirit,"‡ and this life-
giving power lay in His Flesh. S. Athanasius writes,
"The Lord's Flesh is life-giving Spirit,"§ can it be said that
It profiteth nothing?

Nor does "the flesh" ever mean the letter of the law as
distinguished from the spirit, as some have endeavoured to
prove; there is not one passage in Holy Scripture where
it is so employed. I have counted more than fifty passages
in the New Testament in which "*the* flesh" means the con-
dition of man unaided by grace and corrupted by sin and full
of evil propensities, and not one can I find where "*the* flesh"
is used as "the letter" as opposed to the spirit or meaning,
or where it is employed in any good or holy sense, such as
could in any way attach to the Flesh of the Son of God.
Strange interpretation of His words to make Him say that
His Flesh profiteth nothing when He had but just said *It was*
"*Meat indeed*," and that He would give It "for the life of the
world." But it will be asked, why should He allude to His
Ascension? why, but because He would *then* shew how *His*
Flesh differed from "*the* flesh," for It would rise up to
Heaven before their eyes, and the Flesh of the Second
Adam would then become the fountain of Grace to purify
the flesh of the children of the first Adam.

---

* Gal. v. 16.　　† Gal. v. 19.　　‡ 1 Cor. xv. 45.
§ De Incarn. et cont. Ar. § 18, T. i. P. 2 p. 883.

It was when "He ascended up on High, that He led cap tivity captive, and gave gifts unto men"*—the Pentecosta gifts—the Gift of the Holy Ghost, whereby the powers o His Incarnation, till then wrapped up within Himself, wer for the first time in their fullest sense poured out upo His brethren. He Himself gave His Body and Bloo when on earth to His disciples the night before Hi Passion, but He now employed *them* to give that sam gift to all mankind though *He* was in Heaven; there wa no Eucharist that we read of celebrated by the Apostle between our Lord's Passion and the day of Pentecost; i was on that day men knew for the first time the ful meaning of His words, "What and if ye shall see the So of Man ascend up where He was before—it is the Spiri that quickeneth, the flesh profiteth nothing, the words tha I speak unto you, they are spirit and they are life." The also understood they His other words—" He that believet on me the works that I do, shall he do also, and *greate works then these* shall he do, *because I go unto my Father.*"† When He spoke these words He had not celebrated th Holy Eucharist Himself, but after His Ascension He woul entrust that wondrous power to His disciples—this would be a "greater work" than any He had yet done, but n other work of theirs was ever greater than the miracle He had already performed. It was for this reason tha He connected His Ascension with the gift of the Holy Eucharist.

Thus it was that S. Augustine, S. Cyril, and othe ancient Fathers, understood our Lord's words; never a though "the flesh that profiteth nothing" was the precious Body of our Lord.

It is sometimes urged that the absence of the word

* Eph. iv. 8. † S. John xiv. 12.

"Altar" from the Prayer-book proves that the Church of England no longer holds the Catholic doctrine of the Blessed Sacrament. Those who argue thus can hardly be aware that the term which the Church of England does employ, viz., "The Lord's Table," is always used in the Old Testament in a sacrificial sense, as equivalent to the word "altar." For example, in Malachi i. 7, we read, "Ye offer polluted bread upon mine altar; and ye say, Wherein have we polluted Thee? In that ye say the table of the Lord is contemptible." Again, in Ezekiel xli. 22, we read, "The altar of wood was three cubits high, and the length thereof two cubits; *** and he said unto me This is the table that is before the Lord." The ancient liturgies of the primitive Church use both words, "altar" and "table;" for example, the liturgy of S. James, which is the oldest one that has come down to us, uses "altar" fifteen times, and "table" twice, while the liturgy of S. Chrysostom, which is a good deal later, having been compiled about A.D. 400, uses "altar" three times, and "table" seventeen times. In fact, the word "table" implies all that the word "altar" implies, and something more. The word "altar" looks exclusively to the sacrificial aspect of the Holy Eucharist, whilst the word "table" implies that it is both a Sacrifice and a Sacrament. And so S. Paul speaks of "the Table of the Lord," and at the same time tells us "we have an Altar" to which no unconverted Jew should be suffered to approach—"whereof (he says) they have no *right* to eat which serve the tabernacle."

The word "faithful" in the Catechism, where it is said, that "the Body and Blood of Christ are verily and indeed taken and received *by the faithful* in the Lord's Supper," is often relied upon as an argument against the doctrine of the Real Presence—for it seems to say that not

every Christian who receives Holy Communion "tak
and receives" the Body and Blood of Christ, but only
faithful few out of the general number of Communicani
It is sufficient answer to this to refer to the XIXth Artic
which states that " The *Visible Church of Christ* is a cc
" gregation of *faithful* men, in the which the pure Wo
" of God is preached, and the Sacraments be duly min
" tered according to Christ's ordinance in all those thin
" that of necessity are requisite to the same."

Now "the Visible Church of Christ" must mean the
persons who are in *Visible* Communion with the Catho
Church, and not those who are in some sort of invisil
Communion, the result of peculiar sanctity, or some decr
of Election. We must bear in mind that in the old la
guage, a heathen would be called " an infidel" (infidelis
a Christian, a faithful man (fidelis), and yet the heath
might be a better man than the Christian; *we* use t
word in a different sense, comparing Christians wi
Christians of whom we call some " faithful," and othe
" unfaithful," but such was not the language of our foi
fathers—they called all men in Visible Communion wi
the Church " faithful men" (fideles); all men who we
not in Communion with the Church " infidels," (in
deles). In the Communion office when " the blessed coi
" pany of all faithful people " is spoken of, it is not
select few that are meant, but the Visible Church
Christ—so, also, in the Article, so, too, in the Catechism

But people say, Yes, it may be true that the Communi
Service and the Catechism appear to teach the doctrine
the Real Presence, but we must explain the Prayer-boi
by the Articles, and the XXVIIIth Article distinctly asser
that " The Body of Christ is given, taken, and eaten
the Supper *only* after an heavenly and spiritual manner
Now the first part of this statement, if we will only atter

to it, contains a most strong assertion of the doctrine of the Real Presence; for it declares that Christ's Body is not only " eaten " by the communicant, but also " given " by the priest. It is first in the hands of the priest who " gives " It, then in the hands of the communicant who " takes " It, and not till then is It " eaten," as in the Catechism It is said to be " taken and received," taken in the hand, received into the mouth.*

But then we are told that the latter part of the above sentence from the XXVIIIth Article destroys the force of the former part, and that the words " heavenly and spiritual " mean the same as figurative and unreal. Now such an argument would betray a disbelief in every thing which can not be perceived by the senses. The mode of existence by which the soul exists in the body, is a spiritual mode of existence, but is it therefore at all figurative or unreal? Surely not. The soul does not exist in the body by a material or corporal way of existing, and yet we know and are sure that it is there. The assertion that our Lord's Body is present in the Blessed Sacrament " after an heavenly and spiritual manner," would be admitted even by Roman Catholics, who hold the doctrine of Transubstantiation.

---

* It is replied that the Article says, "the means whereby the Body of " Christ is received and eaten in the Supper is Faith."

Yes, Faith by all means, what I am combatting is not Faith but unbelief; men will not believe Christ's plain words, and dignify their unbelief by the name of Faith. I believe Christ can do anything that He says He will do; you say He could not do what He said He did. Which is Faith and which is unbelief?

A blind man was asleep in a burning house, and one ran into his bedroom, roused him up, and told him that the house was on fire, and that there was a fire-escape at the window by which he could reach the ground; he believed what he was told, was led to the window, helped on to the fire-escape, and reached the ground in safety. If he had not believed in the danger, or that the fire-escape was there, he would have been burned to death, so that he was saved by *believing*, that is, by Faith; but was he not also saved by the fire-escape? would his Faith have sufficed without the fire-escape, nay, was not the

For example, Cardinal Bellarmine, the great Roma controversialist, says :—

" So then we shall say, that Christ is in the Eucharie " 'truly, really, substantially,' but we shall not say 'co " 'porally,' *i.e.*, in that manner in which bodies exist of the " own nature, nor ' sensibly, moveably, &c.' Yea, it migl " be said, on the contrary, that He is there ' spiritually,' ɛ " Bernard saith in the sermon on S. Martin."*

But we have a still stronger proof that this clause of tl XXVIIIth Article was never meant to deny the doctrine ι the Real Presence. A letter is preserved in the State Papι Office, (Domestic correspondence, T. xli. No. 51), froɔ Bishop Geste, of Rochester, (the writer of the XXVIIIt Article) to Sir William Cecil, the Prime Minister of the da; in which he utterly denies that the meaning which is no attempted to be forced upon his words, was the meanin which he had when he wrote them. This is a very ir portant document, and one would think that no hone; person, after reading it, will say that the XXVIIIth Artic commits the Church of England to a denial of the Re Presence.

---

fire-escape the very thing believed in, and on which Faith rested, and by whi the man escaped through Faith? and surely the Faith of him who believes the Holy Eucharist as God's saving gift is no more to be set against ti Eucharist itself, than the blind man's Faith is to be set against the fire-escaɪ

And so the Homily speaks of Faith as "a necessary instrument in all the holy ceremonies," and it adds : "It is well known that the meat we seek " this Supper is spiritual food, the nourishment of our soul, a heavenly refecti- " and not earthly, an invisible and not bodily, *a ghostly substance* and not carn: " So that to think that without Faith we may enjoy the eating and drinkiɩ " thereof, or that *that* is the fountain of it, is but to dream of a gross carɛ " feeding, basely objecting and bending ourselves to the elements and creatureɛ The Body and Blood of Christ is received by Faith and not by sense or sigl because, as Bishop Geste puts it, one "cannot see It, smell It, or taste It," aɪ It can only be recognized by Faith, because It is not perceptible by senɟ This is to "discern the Lord's Body," but, as already stated, Faith discerns th which *is*, not that which *is not*.

* Bellarmine de Eucharistiâ ii. 2.

It runs, as follows :—

' Greeting in ye Lord.

" Right Honourable.—I am verye sorye yt [that] you
ire so sicke, God make you whole, as it is my desyer and
)rayer.   I wold have seen you er this, according to my
.luetye and good will, but when I sent to knowe whether
: might see you, it was often answered yt you were not
o be spoken with.

" I suppose you have heard how ye Bisshop of Glocesre
(*i.e.* Cheney) found him selue [himself], greeved with
re plasynge of this adverbe *onelye* in this Article: ' The
Body of Christ is gyven, taken and eaten in ye Supper
after an heavenly and spirituall manner *only*, bycause it
lid take awaye ye presence of Christis Bodye in ye Sacrament, and privily noted me to take his part therein, and
yeasterday in myn absence more playnely vouched me
or ye same.   Whereas betweene him and me, I told him
playnely that this word *onelye* in ye foresaed Article did
iot exclude ye presence of Christis Body from the Sacra-
nent, but only ye *grosseness and sensibleness* in ye receavinge
hereof: For I saied unto him though he tooke Christis
Bodye in his hand, received It with his mouthe, and that
corporally, naturally, reallye, substantially, and carnally
us ye doctors doo write, yet did he not for all that see It,
feale It, smell It, nor tast It.   And therefore I told him I
wold speake against him herein, and ye rather bycause ye
Article was of myn owne pennynge.   And yet I wold
iot for all that denye therebye anything that I had
spoken for ye Presence.   And this was ye some [sum] of
)ur talke.

" And this that I saied is [held] so true by all sortes
)f men, that even D. Hardinge writeth ye same, as it
appeareth most evidently by his wordes, reported in ye
Busshoppe of Salisburie's (Jewel's) booke, *pagina* 325,

which be these: 'Then ye maye saye, yt in ye Sacra-
‚'ment His verye Bodye is present, yea really, that is to
'saye, in deede, substantially, that is in Substance, and
ᶦ corporally, carnally, and naturally; by ye which words
'is ment that His verye Bodye, His verye Flesh, and
'His verye Human Nature is there, not after corporall,
'carnall, or naturall wise; but invisibly, unspeakeably,
'supernaturally, spiritually, divinely, and by waye unto
'Him onlye knowen.'

"This I thought good to write to your honour for mine
owne purgation. The Almighty God in Christ restore
you to your old health," &c.*

Another place which is brought up to prove that the
Church of England denies the doctrine of the Real Presence

---

* The Corporal Presence of Christ's Body would be a tautology as much as the
bodily presence of Christ's Body would be, if by Corporal Presence was meant
the same as Real Presence; but if corporal be distinguished from a spiritual
and immaterial but yet Real Presence, so as to mean some gross or sensible
Presence, then the Corporal Presence of Christ's Body is not a tautology; of
course the word Corporal Presence may simply mean the presence of a body,
though it be a Spiritual Presence, but it may also mean a gross or sensible
Presence; and it is thus we must reconcile the seeming contradiction in Bishop
Geste's letter, when after allowing (as it would seem), twice over, that Christ
was "*corporally*" present in the Eucharist, he yet adds "*not after corporal,
carnal or natural wise*," meaning, as he says, not to "exclude the Presence of
Christ's Body from the Sacrament, but only the grossness and sensibleness in
the receiving thereof."

We have seen that in this latter meaning even Bellarmine says that "Christ
" is in the Eucharist, but we shall not say '*corporally*,' that is, in the manner in
" which bodies exist of their own nature," and that this is the meaning of the
words "Corporal Presence" in the Rubric is the more plain, from the words
that follow, that the "Natural Body and Blood of Christ are in Heaven, and
" not here;" to doubt this would be heresy.

And it is well known that after some time the Lutherans fell into this very
heresy, of thinking that our Lord in Heaven has no Natural Body; that His
Human Body, which was born of a pure Virgin, crucified, dead, and buried, is
in no sense locally in Heaven, whither He was seen to ascend, but that as we
speak of the Godhead as being Omnipresent, so His manhood is to be thought
Omnipresent also, and not merely present by His will in the Holy Eucharist,
and because He wills it, but by *necessity*, owing to the union of the Godhead
and the manhood in One Person. In his later years Luther writes: "The

s the Declaration on kneeling at the end of the Communion Service.

Therein it is asserted, that by the posture of kneeling t was never intended to imply that any adoration was to be given, either to the Sacramental Bread and Wine, (a thing vhich no one ever imagined), or to "any Corporal Presence of Christ's natural Flesh and Blood."

Now it is to be observed here, that this Declaration was irst put into the Prayer-book by King Edward VI on his own authority, without the consent of Parliament or Con-vocation, and that when he put it in, it denied that adora-ion was to be given to "any *Real and Essential* Presence of Christ's natural Flesh and Blood." When Elizabeth came to the throne, the Declaration was expunged from

---

Body and Humanity of Christ are within and without all creatures, as God Himself is. For since Christ is one individual Person, wheresoever He is according to His Divinity, there He also is at the same time, according to His Humanity, or our Faith is false." He even says: "He is present in all creatures" (viz., by His Humanity), "so that I could find Him in straw, fire, water, &c. He fills all things' 'in this way' (as has been acutely observed), while thinking He was defending the Real Presence, He was in reality abandoning it."

Brenz, who was one of His disciples, says that our Lord did not locally scend in His ascension; that the Right Hand of God, where the apostle saith He ath sat down, is everywhere; that His manhood was in Heaven as soon as it as in the Virgin's womb, and that it is now in common household bread as iuch as in the Holy Eucharist. He writes: "I have at home bread and wine in which the Body and Blood of Christ are present, and I may take them every day, yea, every hour. But hear thou in turn: Although Christ in His Majesty together with His Body and Blood is no wise absent from the household bread and wine, yet that thou mayest receive it efficaciously the word of Christ is to be followed."

So that we see it was a very necessary doctrine upon which to insist that The Natural Body and Blood of our Saviour Christ are in Heaven, and not here," for the Reality of the supernatural Presence of His Body and Blood ere, depends upon the Reality of His Natural Body and Blood there, and issues rom Them, and of course it is against the truth of Christ's Natural Body in Ieaven to be at one time in more places than one, but this is no denial of His upernatural but Real and Essential Presence in the Holy Eucharist, wherever t is celebrated.

the Prayer-book as having no ecclesiastical authority, and it was not again printed in the Prayer-book for more than a hundred years. At the last revision of the· Prayer-book in 1662, the Puritans requested that this Declaration should be restored. The Bishops at first declined, but afterwards they put in the Declaration with one important alteration, instead of the words " Real and Essential," they inserted the word " Corporal." " Plainly, the word Corporal, which " they admitted, could not in their minds imply the same " as the words Real and Essential, which they rejected;" " it "is a mere absurdity to say that they meant the same, as " if they had left in what they struck out, and left out what " they put in." *

Whatever, therefore, the Declaration denies, it does not deny that adoration is due to the *Real and Essential* Presence of Christ's Flesh and Blood.

In fact both the epithets " Corporal " and " Natural" refer not to the Presence Itself but to the mode of the Presence. What is meant is that our Lord's Flesh and Blood are not present in a corporal and natural way as they are in heaven, but in a spiritual and supernatural way, as we have already shown they are in the Blessed Sacrament.

And that this was really the intention of the Bishops in 1662, we are further assured by their own published statements concerning their belief in the Real Presence.

Bishop Cosin was the principal reviser, and in his history of Transubstantiation, p. 53, we find these words :—

" Where is the danger, and what doth he fear, as long " as all they that believe the Gospel own the true nature " and the Real and Substantial Presence of the Body of " Christ in the Sacrament."

---

* E. B. Pusey, D.D., reply to Mr. Goode, p. 224.

Bishop Sparrow, another reviser, tells us that the com-municant ought to answer Amen after the words of administration, " by this ' Amen ' professing his faith of " the Presence of Christ's Body and Blood in that Sacra-" ment."—*Rationale of the Book of Common Prayer, p.* 220 ; and in p. 236, he says :—

" It is to be given to the people kneeling, for a sin it is not to adore when we receive this Sacrament." "And the old custom was to receive It after the manner of adoration." For which he quotes S. Augustine and S. Cyril.

Dr. Thorndike, was another reviser, and his testimony to the Catholic doctrine of the adoration of our Lord present in the Blessed Sacrment, has been quoted in the first sermon, p. 24.

It is simply impossible to believe that these learned and pious dignitaries of the Church could have had a hand in imposing on the Church a formulary which contradicted their own most firm belief.

Thus have I endeavoured to answer every objection that seemed worth the least attention against the doctrine of the Real Presence of Christ in Holy Communion. If I have omitted any objection, it was not because I feared to face it, for I am sure there are none stronger than those I have considered. I have stated them for the most part in the words of those who oppose the doctrine, that I might state them with the greater fairness ; my object in preaching these sermons has been to supply you, my brethren, with an answer to gainsayers, which seemed especially needed at the present time, when such fierce attacks are being made against what was always the central doctrine of the Faith, the doctrine of the Incarnation, and against that which is its expression and application on earth, the doctrine of the Real Presence of Christ in Holy Communion. They who oppose that doctrine do not always see that this is really a question of belief or unbelief, Infidelity or the Faith. The Holy Eucharist is the great outwork of Christianity, (to use a military phrase) on the defence of which all depends, when that outwork is carried the rest is only a question of time, it may even take generations to complete the overthrow, but at last all faith goes with it. The doctrine of the Incarnation collapses at once, for under no pretence of reason can a man admit the Incarnation and deny any miracle if only God have revealed it. The Supernatural disappears from Religion, Natural Religion takes the place of revealed, and there might as well have been no Christ born at Bethlehem and cradled in a manger, sweating Bloody Sweat in Gethsemane, crucified on Calvary. It is in this sacrament especially, that the Lord Jesus, though sitting at God's right hand, is yet our "Emmanuel" or "God with us;" this is the link that unites the two worlds, the spiritual and the material, heaven and earth, and that by the secret and subtle transmission to us of His Spiritual Substance Who is the Lord of both worlds, for as God and Man He belongs to both.

Man by his ingenious mechanism can transmit through the abyss of the ocean the subtle force of the electric fluid, and, in an instant, 4,000 miles away; it appears there, as it were, a living power in two Continents at the same moment—flashing from the hard, cold metal which has become its momentary residence. Who would not have called this a physical impossibility a few years ago?

And shall it be thought impossible for Him, who in His own Person unites both worlds as God and Man, to transmit to us through outward means in The Holy Eucharist the subtle substance of that sacred Manhood which He has for ever united to His Godhead. I have shown you that our Lord promised to do this—that the Church of the first ages believed that He did so—that our own English Church believes that He still does so. In the defence of this faith may God enable me to live, in the comfort of this faith to close my eyes in death.*

---

* The Rubric preceding the Communion of the Sick is sometimes relied upon as a proof that the Church does not hold what she teaches elsewhere so plainly. "If a man, either by reason of extremity of sickness, or for want of "warning in due time to the Curate, or for lack of company to receive with him, "or by any other just impediment, do not receive the Sacrament of Christ's "Body and Blood, the Curate shall instruct him that if he do truly repent him "of his sins, and stedfastly believe that Jesus Christ hath suffered death upon the "Cross for him, and shed His Blood for his redemption, earnestly remembering "the benefits he hath thereby, and giving Him hearty thanks therefore, he doth "eat and drink the Body and Blood of our Saviour Christ profitably to his "soul's health, although he do not receive the Sacrament with his mouth." Now this very doctrine as to the Spiritual Communion of the Sick was taught in the Sarum Manual before the Reformation, and was held by the Roman Church to be consistent with a belief in Transubstantiation, and therefore the same doctrine as to the Spiritual Communion of the Sick, when taught by the Church of England, can hardly be said to be inconsistent with a belief in the Real Presence.

After stating some reasons which might disable a sick man from communicating, the Sarum Manual goes on to say: "In which case let the Priest say to the sick man: 'Brother, in this case true Faith and good will sufficeth thee, only believe, and thou hast eaten.'" Even the Council of Trent speaks of persons "who, through the wish (voto), eating that Heavenly Bread, feel its fruit and "benefit;" but what does all this mean but what has so often been said, that God is not tied to Sacraments, although He has tied us to them. He is not so bound by His own ordinance that He cannot take the will of a poor sinner for the deed, and give to him who wished for the Sacrament the grace of the Sacrament without Its bodily reception.

At the same time it ought not to be forgotten that, at the time the Rubric was written, the whole adult population were obliged, by law, to communicate three times in the year at least, so that the case contemplated would not, probably, be that of a person who had never received the Sacrament, in a bodily way, with his mouth.

₊ **Many parts of this Sermon were omitted in delivery for want of time.**

APPENDIX A.

I cannot avoid entering an indignant protest against the unfairness of this writer,* of which this instance is only a sample—in page 8, section 6 of this work to which he refers, viz. " Transubstantiation; or thoughts on the change " consequent on consecration in the Lord's Supper, by an English Church." I read, " High Churchmen dwell with laudable emphasis on the Real Presence," and the whole work is an exhortation to them to *add* to *this* doctrine the doctrine of Transubstantiation, and this is brought forward as the proof that they had already done so! Criticizing the writings of High Churchmen, the writer quoted by Mr. Tapson, says, (p. 36), "If any one " will take the trouble to examine the writings, even of those *who believe in the* " *perfect presence of Bread and Wine—together with the Divine Substance*, he " will find a multitude of phrases, which ill accord with such an opinion," so this writer imagines—but is this a proof that the writers criticized by him, *did not believe "in the perfect presence of Bread and Wine with the Divine Sub-* " *stance*," the very thing he finds fault with, or in other words, is this a proof that they *did* believe in Transubstantiation. In page 37, after quoting from the writings of those whom Mr. Tapson calls Ritualists, this writer says, " Here " lest it should be thought that the works from which these passages are taken, " accept Transubstantiation, I must state that many of them are *expressly* " averse to it," and it is not even hinted that any of them admit it, and yet this writer is the witness called by Mr. Tapson, to prove that we *do* teach it. In p. 37. he says that " the coexistence of the two Substances is sometimes compared to " the mystery of the Incarnation," in which the Substance of God is combined with the substance of man—and this is the proof—that we hold a doctrine, " not to be distinguished from the doctrine of the Council of Trent," which declares the substance of the Bread and Wine to be abolished, In p. 44 ; the writer quoted by Mr. Tapson, writes, " I once more repeat, that my object is simply this : to " suggest that *we* [i.e., High Churchmen] may have been *over hasty in our con-* " *demnation* of belief in a complete change of Substance, and to remind men that " if we could make a few slight alterations, or even make a few omissions, we " should have, *in addition to the pleasure of correcting ourselves*, the pleasure of " harmonizing better with other Catholics." This is a modest proposition from a man who confesses, page 22, that " he can lay no claim to direct acquaintance " with Patristic theology." My former Sermon will have shown you that we should not harmonize better with the great divines of the English Church by adopting Transubstantiation, as this writer proposes : and men who *can* lay

* Rev. R. Tapson, ut supra, p. 7.

claim to direct acquaintance with the writing of the early Fathers, tell us we should not better harmonize with the primitive Church by adopting that doctrine, (see page 13 of this Sermon). It is evident that this author, whoever he may be, represents nobody but himself, indeed he says so plainly, and yet on the strength *of the Title of his book*, he is referred to as representing all those whom Mr. Tapson is pleased to call Ritualists, and whom on this evidence he accuses of teaching Transubstantiation!

Another instance of his unfairness is this, he first caricatures the Roman Church, *accusing her of what she never taught*, and then holds up the picture he he has drawn, and says it is the likeness of High Churchmen. I deny that it is even the likeness of Roman Catholics. For example, Mr. Tapson amuses himself by imagining the possibilities whereby a devout soul who believed in Transubstantiation, or (what he calls the same thing) the Real Presence, might commit the sin of idolatry, by offering adoration to the elements instead of Christ, Christ not being sacramentally Present when that poor soul thought He was Present. He informs us that " it is held that various accidents prevent the miracle of Tran-" substantiation, "or (as I would express it) of the Real Presence." If, for example, " there is any defect in the Priest, if there is any break in the chain of his " succession from the Apostles, or if he does not believe in Transubstantiation," or, as I would again express it, the Real Presence, "if there be any mistake in " the vestments, if the bread be not all of wheaten flour, if the wine be " extracted from any admixture of sour grapes, the Sacrament is not made, " and the deluded worshipper has been guilty of, and is always in danger of, " worshipping a piece of bread as God."*

If this account be true certainly there is very serious peril here. There are very many Priests who do not seem to believe in their own office, especially that which is the chief part of it—to dispense the Body and Blood of Christ to their people, and teach them the powers that belong, and the responsibilities that attach to that most Heavenly Gift, for It is a " savour of death unto death," or a " savour of life unto life." Mistakes in the vestments are undoubtedly common in many of our Churches. Our baker's bread is not always pure, so that it is as well to do as we do in this Church, viz., to have bread specially prepared for that holy use. Certainly it is possible that there may have been some admixture, ever so slight, of sour grapes in the wine, and you, poor soul, who went to adore and receive your Lord, have not only missed the Precious Gift of His Presence, but have insulted Him in His Absence by worshipping a bit of bread.

It is no business of mine to defend the Roman Missal, but I venture to think that the Missal does not say that there is no true Sacrament " if there be any mistake in the vestments," or " if the bread be not all of wheaten flour," or "if the wine be extracted from any admixture of sour grapes." No doubt the Missal gives directions as to all these matters, and many others, in the Chapter, "de defectibus in celebratione missarum occurrentibus," but in the very first clause, which this writer could never have read, it is declared that although such

---

* Rev. R. Tapson.

minute care ought to be used, and so many things attended to, yet only *thre* *things are absolutely essential* to the validity of the Sacrament—a truly ordained. Priest, true bread and wine, and the form of words appointed by our Lord used with the intention of doing what our Lord commanded to be done whence it appears that though a Priest of the Roman Church would be guilty of a grievous offence in not using the proper vestments, their use is no essential to the Sacrament. In the Acts of the Martyrs mention is made of a Priest lying on the floor of his prison with his feet in the stocks, and using his own breast as an Altar, whereon he celebrated the Holy Mysteries for himsel and his fellow prisoner, about to suffer martyrdom with him. I suppose there were no proper vestments, but I doubt not there was a true Sacrament.*

I do not pretend to be thoroughly acquainted with the Missal, but I have searched in vain for any passage that would even seem to assert that *any* mistake, however great, much less however slight, in the vestments would invalidate the Sacrament, or that if the Priest did not believe in Transubstantiation there would be no Sacrament. I confess I have rather lost confidence in the quotations of this writer, to whom I have referred so often, and I have some curiosity to learn what passages he alludes to. Neither vestments nor belief in Transubstantiation are mentioned when the three things *are* mentioned which alone are said to be essential, and certainly it does not seem as if the validity of the Sacrament depended much on the disposition of the Priest when I read: "If a suspended or excommunicated or degraded Priest, or one incapable of " holding office in the Church through some past offence (irregularis), or a " Priest *under any other Canonical impediment*, shall celebrate, he does indeed " celebrate a true Communion, but he sins most grievously, &c." I give the Latin below, headed—"De defectibus dispositionis animae." (Of defects in the disposition of mind of the Priest.)

It is said, indeed, in the Missal that the bread must be wheaten bread, but it is *not* said that the Sacrament fails "if it is not *all* wheaten bread ;" on the contrary, we are told that all that is essential is that it be not "mixed with grains of some other kind *in such quantity* that it no longer remains wheaten bread." Again, we are told in the Missal that the wine should be real wine, but it is added that all that is essential to the Sacrament is that it should not have become " *altogether vinegar*," or " *altogether putrid*," or be *made* of sour grapes, that is, of course, wholly or *chiefly* made of them ; not that "any admixture of sour grapes " accidentally getting into the wine would unfit it for the Sacrament. The plain meaning is, that the bread must be made of ordinary wheaten flour, and the wine must be in the main the fruit of the vine, and that it be such as you could drink yourself without disgust. In the Sacrament of Baptism who would dare to use wine or milk instead of water, when Our Lord said, " baptizing them with water," and what is true of the one Sacrament is true of the other. Our Lord's promise is tied to those elements, and those only, which He Himself appointed to be used, and is this objected to by those who say, " The Bible, the Bible only, and nothing but the Bible!"

---

* Ruinart Tom. iii. p. 182, note.

It may be a *pious* fraud thus to caricature the Roman Missal, but it is a fraud no less. The following are the words of the Missal on the points referred to; I have given their meaning in the above :—

De defectibus in celebratione missarum occurrentibus.

Sacerdos celebraturus, omnem adhibeat diligentiam, ne desit aliquid ex requisitis ad Sacramentum Eucharistiae conficiendum. Potest autem defectus contingere ex parte materiae consecrandae, et ex parte formae adhibendae, et ex parte ministri conficientis. Quidquid enim horum deficit, scilicet materia debita, forma cum intentione, et ordo sacerdotalis in conficiente, non conficitur Sacramentum. *Et his existentibus, quibuscumque aliis deficientibus, veritas adest Sacramenti.* Alii vero sunt defectus, qui in Missae celebratione occurrentes, etsi veritatem Sacramenti non impediant, possunt tamen aut cum peccato, aut cum scandalo contingere.

De defectu panis.

Si panis non sit triticeus, vel si triticeus, *admixtus sit granis alterius generis in tanta quantitate, ut non maneat panis triticeus*, vel sit alioqui corruptus, non conficitur Sacramentum.

De defectu vini.

Si vinum sit *factum penitus acetum* vel *penitus putridum*, vel de uvis acerbis, seu non maturis expressum, vel ei admixtum tantum aquae, ut vinum sit corruptum, non conficitur Sacramentum.

De defectibus dispositionis animae sacerdotis.

Si quis suspensus, excommunicatus, degradatus, irregularis, vel alias canonice impeditus celebret, conficit quidem Sacramentum, sed gravissime peccat, tam propter communionem, quam indigne sumit, quam propter executionem Ordinum, quae sibi erat interdicta.

S. Thomas Aquinas writes :—

" Si sacerdos verba consecrationis proferat super materiâ debitâ cum intentione consecrandi, absque omnibus praedictis, scilicet domo et altari, calice et corporali consecratis, *et caeteris hujusmodi per Ecclesiam institutis* (which would surely include vestments) consecrat quidem in rei veritate Corpus Christi; peccat tamen graviter, ritum Ecclesiae non servans."

Summa Theologica.   Pars III.ia., Qust lxxxiii., Art. iii., 8m.

APPENDIX B.

Speaking of accidents which might happen at the celebration of the Blessed Eucharist, and of the *reverent* care taken to prevent or remedy them, the writer says, "Painful it must be to every reverent (?) mind to hear all this;"* and then he launches out into ridicule of the penances enjoined in days past, and recommended now, in cases where care has not been taken to prevent accidents to the consecrated elements. Are no minds reverent but those which belong to believers in the Real Absence of Christ in Holy Communion? It really seems as if a monopoly of this quality were claimed for them. A belief in the awful Mysteries of the Real Presence of Christ's Body and Blood, causes an exceeding great carefulness to be used at the celebration of them, and then, forsooth pain is felt by *reverent* minds who hear of it! "Reverent minds" are pained at the reverence of other minds! One would have thought it was reverence and that of the most profound kind, which suggested the things complained of. But, no, this is all a mistake; it is not reverence for the Holy Mysteries that causes sorrow or pain when an accident occurs in the celebration of them and induces him whose carelessness caused that accident to submit . to a discipline tending to greater caution in future. No! the reverence is not in him, but in those who hear of his faith and his regret, and turn both into ridicule. And, then, as to the penance. What a dreadful thought! *forty days penance* for spilling a drop of wine. No, not mere wine, but that which is more than wine, that of which Christ said, "This is My Blood." The faith in this makes all the difference. Suppose, now, that every day for forty days the Priest, by whose carelessness the accident occurred, were bidden, as a penance, to read the account of our Lord's Agony and Bloody Sweat; His Cross and Passion; His Institution of the Blessed Sacrament; "This is My Body"— "This is My Blood"—His teaching about it in the sixth of S. John; S. Paul's terrible words about disrespect to It, in the eleventh of 1st Corinthians, and each day to say, "God be merciful to me a sinner;" "O God forgive my thoughtless, careless act." Would this be thought too severe a discipline in such a case? Yet *this* would be a Penance. And is such a Penance as this to be held up to scorn.

---

* Rev. R. Tapson, ut supra, p. 10.

www.ingramcontent.com/pod-product-compliance
Lightning Source LLC
Chambersburg PA
CBHW021437090426
42739CB00009B/1525